CREATIVE EDUCATION

WETLANDS

CHARLES ROTTER

Designed by Rita Marshall
with the help of Thomas Lawton

Published by Creative Education
123 South Broad Street,
Mankato, Minnesota 56001
Creative Education is an imprint
of Creative Education, Inc.

Photography by Gary Braasch, Carr
Clifton, Gerry Ellis, Robert
Llewellyn, Photo Researchers (Bill
Bachman, Francois Gohier, M.H.
Sharp), Tom Stack & Associates
(Matt Bradley, Tom Edwards, Jeff
Foott, Thomas Kitchin, Larry
Lipsky, Brian Parker, Rod Planck),
Larry Ulrich and Visuals Unlimited

Library of Congress
Cataloging-in-Publication Data

Rotter, Charles.
Wetlands / written by Charles
Murray Rotter and Nicole Taylor.
Summary: An introductory book on
wetlands (such as marshes, swamps,
and bogs), their vegetation and
animal life, their benefits to people,
and their need for preservation.
ISBN 0-88682-594-6
1. Wetlands—Juvenile
literature.   2. Wetland ecology—
Juvenile literature.   3. Wetland
conservation—Juvenile literature.
[1. Wetlands.]   I. Taylor, Nicole.
II. Title.   92-41339
QH87.3.R68   1993   CIP
574.5' 26325—dc20   AC

In Memory of
GEORGE R. PETERSON, SR.

7

Millions of years ago, the earth was covered by fertile seas, swarming with marine organisms. As time passed, these sea creatures changed, adapting to new environments. Slowly, some of the marine animals evolved into new forms, able to survive on land. Partially submerged regions called *Wetlands* provided a habitat between the oceans and the land. They served as a transition zone for the migration of life out of the seas and onto the continents.

Low tide at Gambier Bay, Admiralty Island, Alaska.

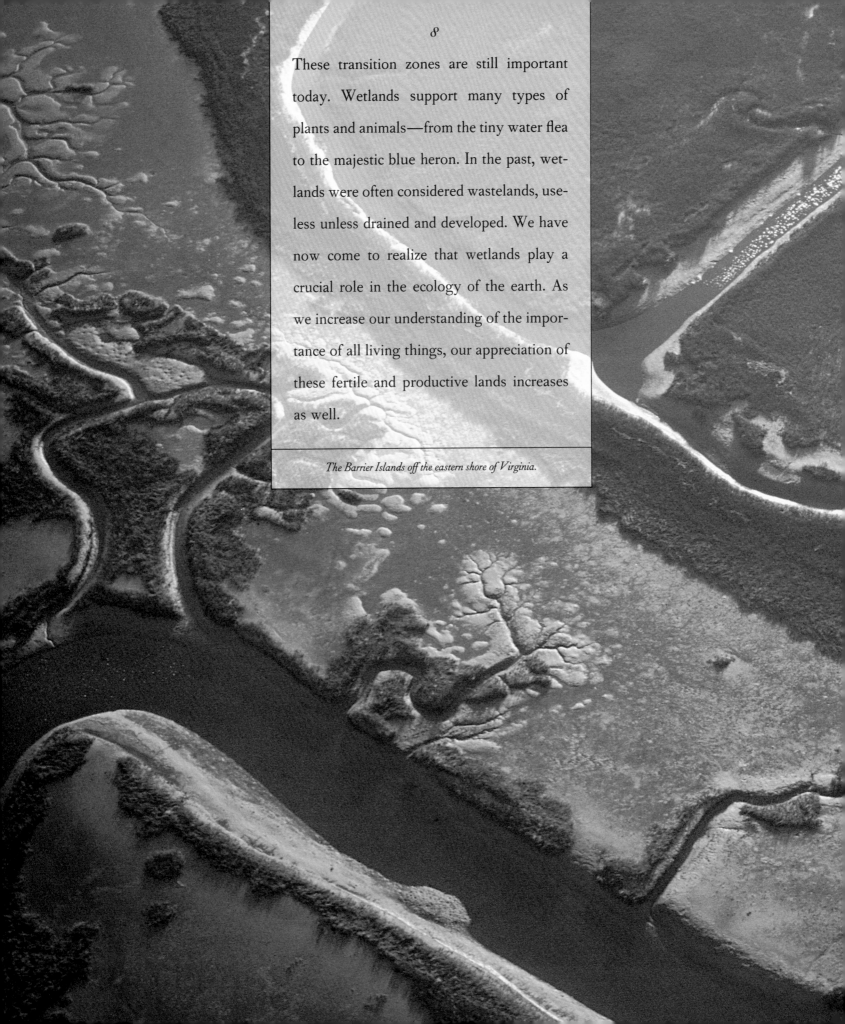

8

These transition zones are still important today. Wetlands support many types of plants and animals—from the tiny water flea to the majestic blue heron. In the past, wetlands were often considered wastelands, useless unless drained and developed. We have now come to realize that wetlands play a crucial role in the ecology of the earth. As we increase our understanding of the importance of all living things, our appreciation of these fertile and productive lands increases as well.

The Barrier Islands off the eastern shore of Virginia.

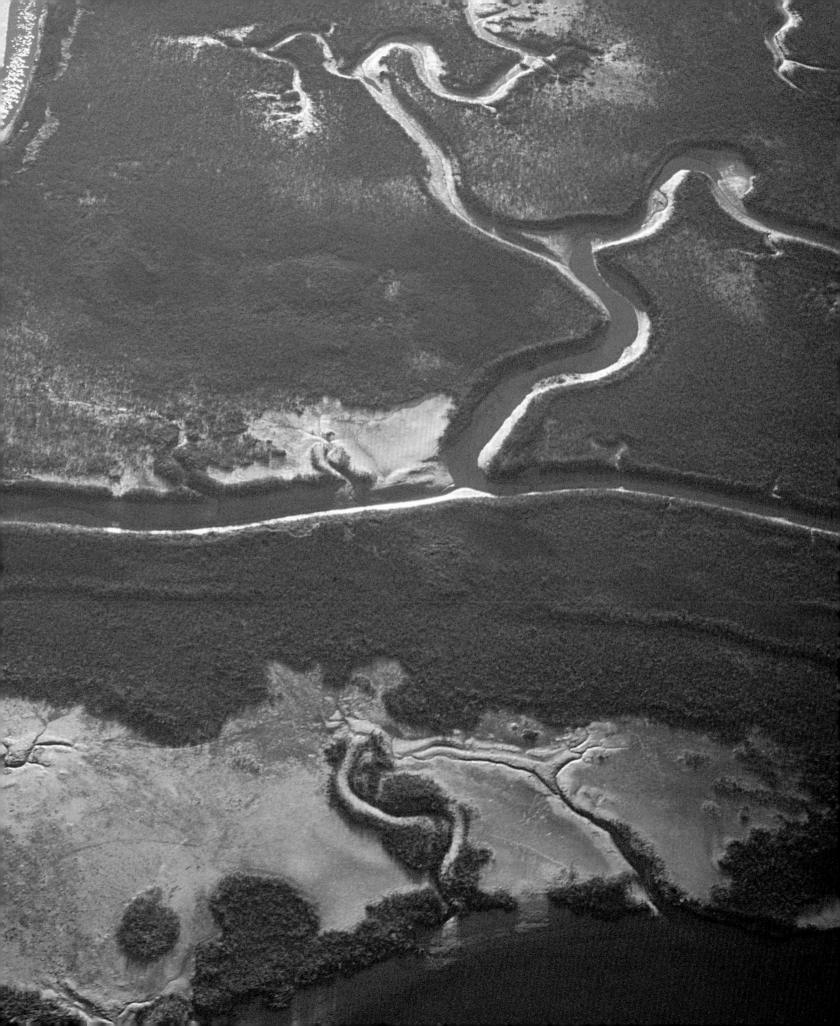

Wetlands are regions on the earth's continents where the *Water Table* (the depth required to reach groundwater) is at or near the surface, or the land is totally submerged up to a depth of 6 feet (1.8 m). There are many types of wetlands, some freshwater, some saltwater, and some that are a mixture of both, called *Brackish* water. Wetlands are classified by their geography, vegetation, soil composition, and amounts and types of water. Classification systems vary widely and are still changing as scientists learn more about wetlands. In this book, non-scientific terms will be used to describe the various wetlands found in the United States and around the world: marshes, swamps, bogs, saltwater marshes, mangrove swamps, and tidal flats. These wetland names sometimes overlap, and one person's swamp may well be someone else's marsh.

A marsh stream in Michigan.

Marshes are common around inland lakes, ponds, and rivers. They are distinguished by their vegetation. Lush plants such as cattails, wild rice, and Jamaican saw grass can be found in marshes. Floating plants, such as fragrant water lilies and tiny duckweed, flourish. Bladderworts and elodea grow beneath the water's surface.

❧

Marshes are one of the most diverse of all wetland communities. Many fish spend all or most of their lives in or near these marshes. Some saltwater fish swim inland into the brackish water of coastal marshes to spawn. Others use marshes as nurseries for juvenile fish, which spend their youth in the relative safety of the dense marsh before venturing out into the open sea. Marshes are also home to many fur-bearing animals, including rabbits, otters, wild boar, and fallow deer. Birds such as herons, egrets, and ducks thrive in marshes as well.

Cattails, a common marsh plant.
Inset: A river otter.

Marshes may form in several ways. Shallow lakes can fill in with sediment and rotting plants, creating a marsh. Other marshes may be found at the shallow water along the sides of rivers, at the edges of lakes, in river flood-plains, or in other areas where shallow water accumulates. Shallow marshes may contain up to 6 inches (15 cm) of water. Deeper marshes have water depths of up to 3 feet (91 cm).

A marsh along the Ohio River, Wayne National Forest, Ohio.

The largest marshland in the world—the Everglades—is located in southern Florida. The Everglades are 50 miles (80 km) wide and more than 100 miles (161 km) long. Famous for alligators, snapping turtles, and abundant waterfowl, the Everglades have nevertheless been harmed by development. Levees built to protect farms and communities from flooding have restricted the flow of water to much of the region, forever altering its ecology. Fortunately, much of the wetland remains in its natural state today, largely due to the creation of the *Everglades National Park*, which protects a marshland larger than the state of Rhode Island.

Everglades National Park, Florida.
Inset: An American alligator.

A *Swamp* is similar to a marsh but has more trees, shrubs, and other woody plants. Frequently, as vegetation in a marsh changes with time, the marsh becomes a swamp. Like marshes, swamps form when water cannot drain out of a depression. Swamp water generally remains anywhere from 1 inch (2.5 cm) to a foot (30 cm) or more deep.

Swamps are known for trees such as red maple, shrubs such as spicebush and sweet pepperbush, and tall plants such as reeds and tall bulrush. Other common plants are the bur reed and the flowering rush. Crocodiles, herons, egrets, wood ducks, and sandhill cranes all make their homes in the swamp. Some of the largest swamplands in the world are near the Pripyat River in the former Soviet Union. Known as the Pinsk Marshes, they cover 18,125 square miles (46,944 sq. km), from northwest Ukraine into southern Belarus.

A cypress swamp.
Inset: Wood ducks.

20

Bogs often bring to mind images of Scottish mystery novels: Hunting dogs chase villains across dense bogs as thick fog rolls over the land. In reality, a bog is a wetland formed in an ancient glacial lake, or in other depressions where the conditions are highly acidic. This acidity prevents the plants that grow there from decomposing, allowing a deep layer of peat to accumulate. On top of this peat, acid-tolerant plants, such as sphagnum moss, dominate the bog. The moss in a bog can be as deep as 40 feet (12 m). Other plants that have found their niche in the bog are pimpernels, orchids, cottons, butterworts, and sundews.

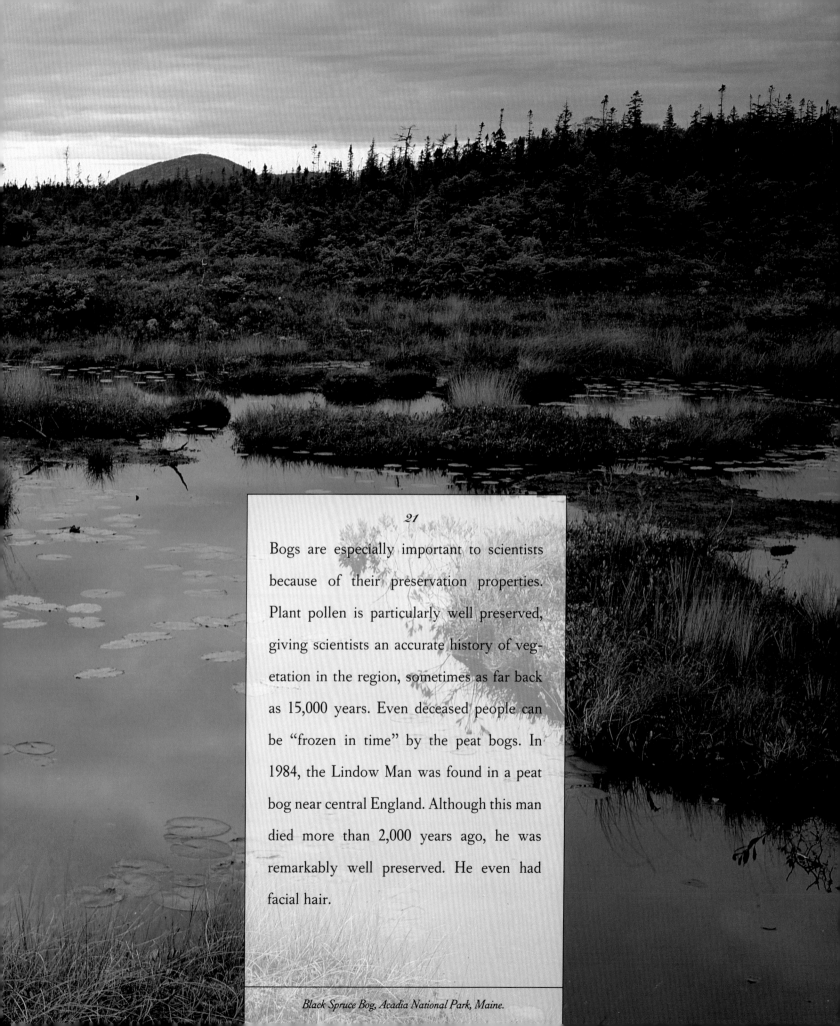

21

Bogs are especially important to scientists because of their preservation properties. Plant pollen is particularly well preserved, giving scientists an accurate history of vegetation in the region, sometimes as far back as 15,000 years. Even deceased people can be "frozen in time" by the peat bogs. In 1984, the Lindow Man was found in a peat bog near central England. Although this man died more than 2,000 years ago, he was remarkably well preserved. He even had facial hair.

Black Spruce Bog, Acadia National Park, Maine.

23

Saltwater Marshes are found along both coasts of the United States, but are much more common along the Atlantic. This is because the coast of the eastern United States has a much shallower slope than that found in the West. The water level in salt marshes fluctuates often with the tides. They have less life than fresh marshes due to the salt in the water and the rapid changes in tides, temperature, and nutrient content. Salt-tolerant grasses such as salt hay grass and needlerush grow in these areas. Near the Pacific, pickleweed, sea blite, and arrow grass are found.

Cornoman Bay on the Potomac River, Virginia.

In tropical latitudes, the salt marsh is re-
placed by the *Mangrove Swamp*. These
swamps are known for their beautiful mangrove trees, whose exposed roots lie above
the soil level but may be submerged in
water. The leaves from the mangrove trees
provide food for microbes, fungi, worms,
and very tiny crustaceans called copepods.
These organisms, in turn, are eaten by crabs,
shrimp, birds, and fish. The brackish waters
of mangrove swamps can be quite salty, or
Saline. The mangrove tree dominates these
wetlands because it is not harmed by saltwater. Mangrove swamps are common in
Florida, New Guinea, Indonesia, Kenya, and
Zaire.

Red mangrove trees in Florida.
Inset: The submerged roots of mangrove trees.

Tidal Flats are another type of wetland. Found on the coasts between the high and low tide points, they are common along the Gulf of Mexico. Their soils are composed of sand, silt, and clay and are regularly exposed to the open air during low tides. The sediments here are not stable and the salinity is high, so there are few plants. Instead, organic debris from nearby salt marshes often collects on the muddy surface. These nutrients provide a food supply for animals living in and around the tidal flats, such as crabs, clams, shrimp, and mussels. These animals then become the food supply for coastal shore birds that hunt the flats, and, during high tides, for fish that live in the surrounding waters.

Shorebirds feeding on crab eggs at Delaware Bay.

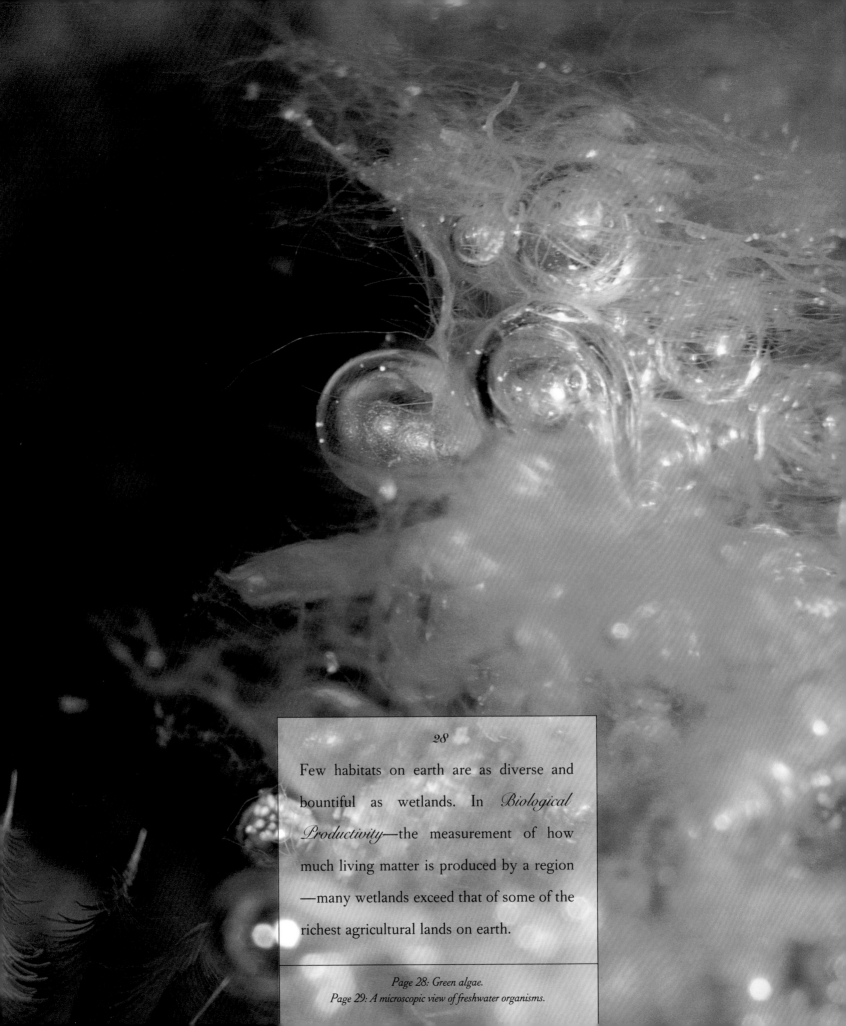

28

Few habitats on earth are as diverse and bountiful as wetlands. In *Biological Productivity*—the measurement of how much living matter is produced by a region —many wetlands exceed that of some of the richest agricultural lands on earth.

Page 28: Green algae.
Page 29: A microscopic view of freshwater organisms.

All energy for life in the wetlands comes initially from sunlight, which passes easily through the shallow waters. In a process called *Photosynthesis*, plants and algae use sunlight to convert air, water, and minerals into carbohydrates, or sugars. These *Producers* of food are in turn eaten by small animals, such as free-swimming larvae called zooplankton, or larger creatures, such as insects, fish, birds, or mammals. These animals are called *Consumers*.

Consumers that in turn eat other consumers are called *Predators*. Alligators are predators. Many wetland birds, such as the pike and the marsh harrier, are predators. An especially ferocious (if not very large) wetland predator is the water beetle, which can eat creatures larger than itself. Other wetland predators are frogs, toads, and fish.

A red-shouldered hawk feeds its young.

Consumers that live off of other consumers without killing them, such as mosquitoes, ticks, and leeches, are known as *Parasites*. These particular parasites will attack people, and while not normally dangerous, they can be quite unpleasant. In many parts of the world, mosquitoes and other parasites spread diseases, including malaria.

A newt eats frog eggs.

In most wetlands, the *Decomposers* complete the food cycle. Bacteria and fungi break down dead animal matter, biological waste, and dead plant material into minerals and nutrients that plants and algae can use to begin the cycle anew.

The wetland ecosystem is vigorous and productive, and its role in supporting wildlife around the world is becoming more evident every year. Approximately 35 percent of all rare and endangered animals in the United States depend on wetlands for their survival —for their habitat, breeding grounds, or food supply. Fish and shellfish are especially susceptible to shrinking wetlands. Without wetlands, many of these creatures will die.

Scallops.

34

Wetlands also have immediate benefits for human life, such as providing flood management for areas bordering them. When a flood occurs, the wetlands absorb the flood waters like a sponge. After the flood is over, they release these waters slowly, in a controlled manner.

During storms, coastal wetland vegetation helps absorb and reduce the energy from waves, lessening the overall effects of the storm. For example, the roots of the mangrove tree hold loose coastal soil in place during hurricanes, preventing the storms from eroding the coastline. These trees can endure major storms without sustaining permanent damage.

The South Slough of Coos Bay, Oregon.

Wetlands also improve water quality. As water flows through a wetland, it slows, and sediments settle to the bottom. The sediments become part of the wetland's soil, and many contaminants in the water are filtered out. The decomposers break down the trapped organic matter and return essential nutrients to the soil and water. Even nitrogen from agricultural fertilizers is released into the atmosphere as safe nitrogen gas.

37

Wetlands are frequently connected to groundwater systems. When people remove water from the systems, excess water from the wetland percolates into the water table, replenishing the groundwater. This is especially useful during droughts, as water from wetlands keeps the groundwater from sinking dangerously low. This supplement to the groundwater helps farmers irrigate their crops and provide water for livestock.

A frozen beaver pond in Colorado's White River National Forest.

Many people still do not appreciate the value of wetlands. Draining and development continue at an alarming rate; every year we permanently lose more of these valuable habitats. In the United States there were once more than 200 million acres (81 million hectares) of wetlands. This number has been reduced by more than half as developers build on the land and drill for oil and gas.

The United States government defines a wetland as an area whose surface is saturated with water from seven to fourteen days annually—long enough for the organisms that live there to adapt to the moist conditions. Developers are lobbying to change the official definition so that fewer lands are classified as wetlands. If the definition of wetlands becomes more restrictive, industry will have more land to develop, and fewer wetlands will be protected. Should this happen, many of the organisms supported by these vital ecosystems will be lost forever.

A marsh oil rig in southern Louisiana.

No one can predict the severity of the damage that will occur if we fail to protect *Wetlands*. We must act now to save these lush environments, essential to life throughout the world.

Hasley Basin near Snowmass, Colorado.